Yeah, I'm a Plant Lady.
(SORRY NOT SORRY!)

KNOCK KNOCK®

LOS ANGELES, CALIFORNIA

T0353115

Created and published by Knock Knock
6695 Green Valley Circle, #5167
Culver City, CA 90230
knockknockstuff.com

ISBN: 978-168349413-3
UPC: 8-25703-50128-5

10 9 8 7 6 5 4 3 2 1

HEY,
PLANT LADY!
YEAH, YOU!

It's trendy to be into plants these days. #Plantlovers have overtaken social media like dandelions in the park. But you're the real deal, plant lady! Your love of horticulture goes way deeper than a hashtag— you've got the calluses, scars, and nursery bills to show it. You paid the cost to be the plant-lady boss.

This book is for you! It's a celebration of your botanical obsession in all its messy, magnificent glory. It embraces and honors your plant-nurturing nature, because guess what? Being a plant lady isn't just hip and cool. It's actually important! Plant ladies fill our lives with magical, life-giving machines that eat poisons and make oxygen (aka plants!). Plant ladies help us breathe better, calm our stressed-out souls, and remind us to stay in touch with our own earthy nature. Plant ladies are missionaries for nature itself.

So let your green-freak flag fly. Of all the plant ladies around, you're the plant-ladiest!

SORRY NOT SORRY!

I secretly judge people who can't keep plants alive.

SORRY NOT SORRY.

My plants have distinct personalities, and I'd be happy to explain them all to you.

Some people have too many purses. I have too many plant cuttings.

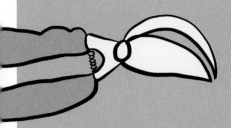

. . . But plant cuttings are basically **FREE PLANTS.** So I'm actually saving money. So they're the opposite of too many purses.

OOPS, I'M FRESH OUT OF SORRY.

PLANT LADY
COMPLIMENTS

- Your spirit is more radiant than a *Helianthus giganteus*!

- Your friendship is like SUPERthrive® solution for my soul.

- You are the only person I would ever trust to plant-sit for me.

- Everyone blossoms in your presence. You're a Mediterranean climate in human form.

- I'd wrestle a *Dracunculus vulgaris* for you!

- Is that an *Amorphophallus* in your pants, or are you just glad to see me?

- After my silver queen plant, I love talking to you the most.

- Your smile could make a Christmas cactus bloom in July.

- You're more cheerful than a morning glory, you smell better than a paperwhite, and you're more fun than a passion flower.

- If I could name a variety of rose after you it would be called *Bestus friendus everus*.

My plants all have names (and nicknames).

SORRY . . . KINDA?

Of course I talk to my plants. They give really good advice.

My idea of a party is wandering the garden section at the home store.

#SNS

That's also my idea
of therapy.

PLANT LADY INSULTS

- I see you're growing thistles and burweed in your yard this year!

- Your garden could be a plant cemetery this Halloween.

- I'd rather hug a stinging nettle than you.

- I'd rather kiss a corpse flower than you.

- You don't kill plants—they die so they don't have to live with you.

- Your soul is drier than cactus potting mix!

- I don't know who's thirstier, you or your elephant ear.

- Do I smell compost? Oh. It's just your breath.

- You're dirty, but in a bad way.

- Your thumb is green—with envy of my garden!

I love animals,
but I kill pests on my plants
with actual vengeance.

IS IT WEIRD THAT I'M SUPER NOT SORRY?

I only give my houseplants filtered water.

YEAH, NOPE. STILL NOT SORRY.

I know the Latin names for my plants. Is that weird?

If I went to Hogwarts, I'd totally volunteer in the Herbology department for extra credit.

Plant pics take up most of the storage on my phone.

REAL TALK: NOT SORRY AT ALL.

People* call me "The Plant Whisperer."

*"People" = mostly me

SORRY TO SAY I'M NOT SORRY!

I've accepted that soft hands and beautiful fingernails are just not a realistic lifestyle choice for me.

JUST OVER HERE NOT SAYING SORRY—SORRY!

PLANT LADY DREAM JOBS

- Resident Groundskeeper at the Palace of Versaille
- Horticulturist at Disneyland
- Arborist at Sherwood Forest
- Plant Hybridizer, Grafter for Monrovia Growers
- Heirloom Seed Preservationist
- Children's Garden Designer
- Lavender Farmer & Beekeeper
- Edible Garden Creator & Instructor
- Tropical Plant Explorer
- Botanical Illustrator

When I'm not home,
I let my plants listen to
their favorite music.

I GOTTA BE ME! SORRY . . . 'NUF SAID.

I always say bye
to my plants
when I leave the house.

○ SORRY ⊗ NOT SORRY

Um, yeah . . .
I also say hi to them
when I get home.

SORRY NOT SORRY.

My plants are like family.
I actually prefer them
to some of my relatives.

SORRY. BUT NOT REALLY.

I enjoy giving my plants "makeovers."

#SORRYNOTSORRY

PLANT LADY PUNS

I'm rooting for you!

Mulch ado about nothing!

I've grown frond of you.

I'll always have thyme for you.

Aloe you vera much.

You had me at aloe.

Honeydew, talk dirt-y to me.

Gee, you sure are a fungi!

Dates make my palms sweat.

Give peas a chance!

I know I sound condescending when I talk about plants with other people, but I'm not. I just know so much more than they do.

SORRY-ISH. (NOT ACTUALLY.)

When I go on trips,
I always wish I could
bring along one or two
of my plants.
(And sometimes I do. Shhh.)

ORRYSAY OTNAY ORRYSAY.

When I travel, I'm more excited about seeing the gardens than the buildings.

WISH I WERE SORRY, BUT . . .

Don't cross me. I know which plants are poisonous. I also know how to make herbal tea. Just sayin'.

SORRY . . . KINDA?

I love succulents, but . . .
they're almost *too* easy.
I enjoy a bit of a challenge,
you know?

Of course I have a favorite plant. I also have a second-favorite, third-favorite, fourth-favorite . . .

SORRY/NOT SORRY

I feel sad when I have to throw away dead flowers. Sometimes I say a few words in honor of their service.

SORRY-ISH. (NOT ACTUALLY.)

PLANT LADY SONGS

"Beechwood Park"
The Zombies

"Big Yellow Taxi"
Joni Mitchell

"Cherry Blossom Girl"
Air

"Crimson and Clover"
Tommy James & the Shondells

"Every Rose Has Its Thorn"
Poison

"Feed the Tree"
Belly

"Garden (Say It Like Dat)"
SZA

"Gardening at Night"
REM

"Honeysuckle Rose"
Fats Waller

"I Built This Garden for Us"
Lenny Kravitz

"Kids"
MGMT

"Lavender Blue (Dilly Dilly)"
Sammy Turner

"Lilac Wine"
Jeff Buckley

"Lilac Wine"
Nina Simone

"(Listen to the) Flower People"
Spinal Tap

"Mercy Mercy Me (the Ecology)"
Marvin Gaye

"Mother Nature's Son"
The Beatles

"Nothing but Flowers"
Talking Heads

"Play in the Sunshine"
Prince

"Roses"
Outkast

"Spanish Harlem"
Ben E. King

"Sugar Magnolia"
The Grateful Dead

"Sunflower"
Harry Styles

"Surprise, Surprise (Sweet Bird of Paradox)"
John Lennon

"The Rose"
Bette Midler

"Tiptoe Through the Tulips"
Tiny Tim

"Tupelo Honey"
Van Morrison

"Who Loves the Sun"
The Velvet Underground

Really good soil smells fresh and *clean.* #IYKYK

OOPS, I'M FRESH OUT OF SORRY.

Sometimes, when I'm in the garden section at a store, people come up and ask me questions about plants. I don't tell them I don't work there.

I genuinely like
the smell of manure.
And blood meal.

SORRY . . . NOT!

. . . And fish emulsion.

YEAH, NOPE. STILL NOT SORRY.

I also think worms are *not* gross, dirty, and squirmy. They're soil-saving superheroes!

SORRY TO SAY I'M NOT SORRY!

And I think bees
and other pollinators are
basically sacred.

REAL TALK: NOT SORRY AT ALL.

PLANT LADY ALBUMS

Stevie Wonder's Journey Through the Secret Life of Plants
Stevie Wonder

Wildflowers
Tom Petty

Parsley, Sage, Rosemary & Thyme
Simon & Garfunkel

The Four Seasons
Antonio Vivaldi

The Rite of Spring
Igor Stravinsky

Mother Earth's Plantasia
Mort Garson

American Beauty
The Grateful Dead

Music to Grow Plants
Dr. George Milstein

Moss Kin
Omni Gardens

Six Songs for Invisible Gardens
Green-House

Some people are addicted to pot. I'm addicted to pots.

SOWWY. *NOT SOWWY.*

. . . But I can stop any time. It's just that my plants keep getting bigger.

IS IT WEIRD THAT I'M SUPER NOT SORRY?

I'm not just a plant parent. I'm a plant rescue-and-rehab facilitator.

JUST OVER HERE NOT SAYING SORRY—SORRY!

I can "hear" my plants telling me when they're thirsty.

ORRYSAY OTNAY ORRYSAY.

PLANT LADY BOOKS

Garden by the Sea ....Mercè Rodoreda

Old Herbaceous .... Reginald Arkell

The Cherokee Rose: A Novel of Gardens and Ghosts .... Tiya Miles

The Garden of Evening Mists ....Tan Twan Eng

The Little Prince ....Antoine de St. Exupery

The Overstory .... Richard Powers

The Secret Garden .... Frances Hodgson Burnett

The Signature of All Things ....Elizabeth Gilbert

Their Eyes Were Watching God .... Zora Neale Hurston

Woman Hollering Creek .... Sandra Cisneros

GARDEN BY THE SEA

The Secret Garden

WOMAN HOLLERING CREEK

I firmly believe you can never have enough plant saucers. (Or enough plants, obvi.)

I GOTTA BE ME! SORRY . . . 'NUF SAID.

Are you going to
throw away those eggshells
and coffee grounds?
I'd be happy to take 'em
off your hands.

SORRY ⊗ NOT SORRY

Have I ever composted poop? No. (Have I thought about it? No comment.)

SORRY/NOT SORRY

I don't just love my plants;
I *respect* them.

If you come to my house and don't compliment my *Monstera deliciosa*,
I won't judge you. I'll assume you need Lasik surgery.

SORRY NOT SORRY.

If you come to my house
and don't notice my orchids,
I won't judge you.
But it will be hard to feel
like you truly understand me.

SORRY. BUT NOT REALLY.

If you come to my house and don't compliment my fiddle-leaf fig, I won't judge you. OK, I might judge you a little bit.

OOPS, I'M FRESH OUT OF SORRY.

PLANT LADY
MOOD BOOSTERS

Sunflowers

Lavender

Rosemary

Chamomile

Basil

Mint

Holy basil/Tulsi

St. John's wort

Roses

Lemon balm

How do I feel about artificial plants? I literally cannot roll my eyes any farther back in my head.

REAL TALK: NOT SORRY AT ALL.

Facts:
Growing super-dazzling,
Insta-ready plants
requires a shocking lack
of sentimentality.
And honesty.

FAVORITE PLANT LADY FLICKS

A Little Chaos (2014)

Adaptation (2002)

Avatar (2009)

Being There (1979)

Bottle Shock (2009)

Enchanted April (1991)

Fairy Tale: A True Story (1997)

Far from the Madding Crowd (2015)

Fern Gully (1992)

Gnomeo & Juliet (2011)

Greenfingers (2001)

Jean de Florette (1987)

Little Shop of Horrors (1986)

Something New (2006)

The Best Exotic Marigold Hotel (2011)

The Constant Gardener (2005)

The Karate Kid (1984)

The Secret Garden (2020)

Wall-E (2008)

Wallace and Gromit: Curse of the Were-Rabbit (2005)

I haven't seriously injured myself with plants, but I've dealt with some roses who were total pricks.

OOPS, I'M FRESH OUT OF SORRY.

. . . And cacti who were clearly hardened criminals.

SORRY . . . KINDA?

When I divide plants, I'm not just dividing plants. I'm creating new family members.

SORRY-ISH. (NOT ACTUALLY.)

People with black thumbs think people with green thumbs must be magic or something. They're not wrong.

THIS IS ME SAYIN' NOT SORRY—JUST SAYIN'...

Some people see a really ugly, half-dead plant about to be tossed in a garbage truck. I see pure potential.

Some people see rotting produce in the refrigerator drawer. I see worm food.

PLANT LADY HALLOWEEN COSTUMES

- **Poison Ivy**

- **Mother Nature**

- **Fairy**

- **Garden gnome**

- **Ladybug**

- **Ophelia**
  (from *Hamlet*)

- **Snow White and Rose Red**

- **Audrey II**
  (killer plant from
  Little Shop of Horrors)

- **Happy little tree**
  (à la Bob Ross)

- **Jolly Green Giant**

Some people see
an empty patch of dirt.
I see soil.
(And cross my fingers
it's not dense clay.)

. . . If it *is* dense clay,
I prep to launch a long-term
guerrilla insurgency.

IS IT WEIRD THAT I'M SUPER NOT SORRY?

PLANT LADY DREAM DESTINATIONS

Aswan Botanical Garden (Egypt)

Butchardt Gardens (British Columbia)

The Hanging Gardens of Babylon
(hey, a person can dream, right?)

Humble Administrator's Garden (Suzhou, China)

Jardim Botanico (Rio de Janeiro, Brazil)

Kenroku-en Garden (Kanazawa, Japan)

Keukenhof (Lisse, the Netherlands)

Kirstenbosch National Botanical Garden
(Cape Town, South Africa)

Las Pozas (Xilitla, Mexico)

Limahuli Garden & Preserve (Kauaʻi, Hawaiʻi)

Longwood Gardens (Kennett Square, Pennsylvania)

Mauritius National Botanical Garden (Mauritius)

Monet's Garden at Giverny (France)

Nong Nooch Tropical Garden (Pattaya, Thailand)

Powerscourt Estate (Ireland)

Pukekura Park (New Zealand)

Redwood Sky Walk, Sequoia Park Zoo (Eureka, California)

Svalbard Global Seed Vault
(Svalbard Island, Arctic Ocean, Norway)

Tortuguero National Park (Costa Rica)

Victoria Falls National Park Rainforest (Zimbabwe)

Some people see chickens. I see magical fertilizer fairies.

Some people see piles of dead leaves. I see free mulch.

Some people see mistletoe and think of Christmas. I think, *toxic tree-killing parasite.*

PLANT LADY NAMES FOR PETS

Violet	Blossom
Buttercup	Daisy
Petunia	Ivy
Primrose	Petal
Flower	Tiger Lily

I'm a proud tree-hugger, and I find that some trees give better hugs than others. (I'd never tell them because it might hurt their feelings.)

SORRY... NOT!

Some people might think
I have too many plant
and gardening books.
These people are idiots.

SORRY. BUT NOT REALLY.

BEST PLANTS FOR GRUMPS

Prickly pear

Stinging nettles

Oleander

Snake plant/
Mother in law's tongue

Venus flytrap

Castor bean

Water hemlock

Deadly nightshade

White snakeroot

Pitcher plant

I can't imagine life without trees. Which is why I could never live in space, or on an aircraft carrier.

My favorite people-names? Lavender, Rose, Lily, Poppy . . .

WISH I WERE SORRY, BUT . . .

My favorite Marvel character? Groot. (Duh.)

My favorite
comic book villain?
Poison Ivy.
(Double duh!)

SORRY/NOT SORRY

PLANT LADY PLANTS FOR THOSE WHO LIKE A CHALLENGE

Orchids

Fiddle leaf fig

Maidenhair fern

Staghorn fern

Artichokes

Venus flytrap

Wasabi

Elephant ear

Cauliflower

Celery

PLANTS TO GIVE TO NON-PLANT PEOPLE

**Beer plant/
Castiron plant**

Pothos

Snake plant/
Mother in law's tongue

Spider plant

Aloe vera

Jade plant

String of pearls

OK, any succulent

ZZ Plant

Heartleaf *philodendron*

I wish I could tell the whole world: stop trying to grow trees from avocado pits! That's not how avocados work. Just trust me.

It's not just payday—
it's an excuse to buy more
plants.

SORRY...NOT!

Some people say
I'm a plant snob . . .
like it's a bad thing.

YEAH, NOPE. STILL NOT SORRY.

If I lived in the Middle Ages, I'd probably be an herbal healer-type with a little garden and a cat. Yeah, I'd basically be a witch.

SORRY TO SAY I'M NOT SORRY!

COMMON PLANTS WITH FANCIFUL NAMES

Love lies bleeding

Adder's tongue

Kangaroo's paw

Jupiter's beard

Wandering Jew

Fishbone cactus/
Ric-rac cactus

Rabbit's foot fern

Jack in the pulpit

Bleeding heart

Beardtongue/
Blackbeard
penstemon

HELLO, MY NAME
Jupiter's
Beard

HELLO, M
Kang
Pa

I was a plant lady
before being a plant lady
was cool.

REAL TALK: NOT SORRY AT ALL.

COMMON PHRASES FROM PLANTS

"Low-hanging fruit"

"Coming up roses"

"Late bloomer"

"Shrinking violet"

"Wallflower"

"Gilding the lily"

"Nip it in the bud"

"Can't see the forest for the trees"

"The grass is always greener on the other side of the fence"

"Growing like a weed"

Some plants have been in my life longer than some friends. (And I'm talking like, close friends.)

THIS IS ME SAYIN' NOT SORRY—JUST SAYIN'...

Obvi, some plants have also lasted longer than some romantic relationships. (And been more rewarding, come to think of it.)

SOWWY. *NOT SOWWY.*

People think gardening looks peaceful, but it's full of drama, sex, danger... but like, on a bug-size scale.

IS IT WEIRD THAT I'M SUPER NOT SORRY?

Like people, plants can be hard to please. Unlike people, they never vibe you about it.

ORRYSAY OTNAY ORRYSAY.

Also, plants don't care
if I've brushed my teeth,
or put on pants.

I GOTTA BE ME! SORRY . . . 'NUF SAID.

Houseplants absorb toxic fumes, produce oxygen and negative ions, and improve chi flow. They're like a spiritual guru crossed with an air conditioner.

JUST OVER HERE NOT SAYING SORRY—SORRY!

I'm not saying plants are better than people, but . . . **PLANTS ARE BETTER THAN PEOPLE.**

THE END